This book belo

_____

My Chinese name is

_____

Hi, I'm Fabio. Let's start learning.

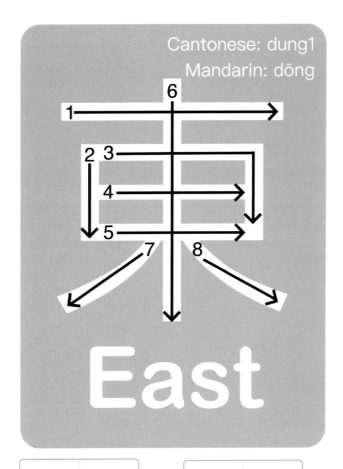

Cantonese: dung1
Mandarin: dōng

East

Which direction does the sun rise?

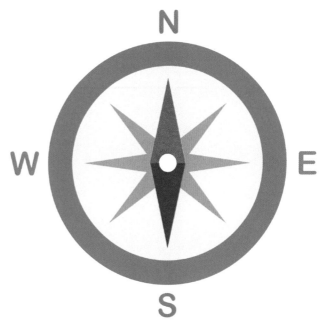

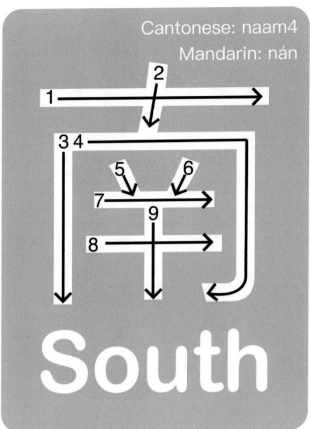

Cantonese: naam4
Mandarin: nán

South

Name a country in the Southern Hemisphere

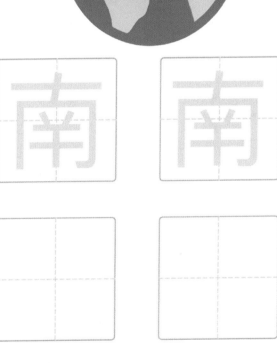

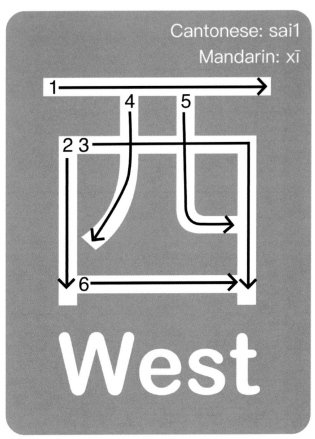

Cantonese: sai1
Mandarin: xī

West

Which direction does the sun set?

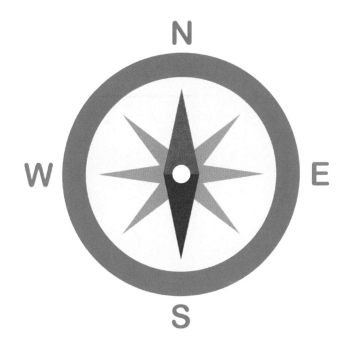

N

W   E

S

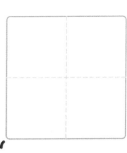

Cantonese: bak1
Mandarin: běi

North

Name a country in the
Northern Hemisphere

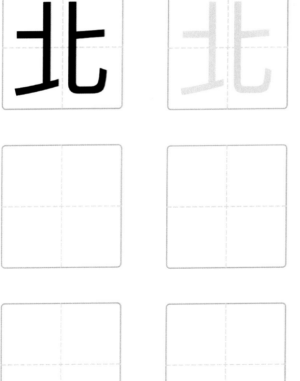

Cantonese: loi4
Mandarin: lái

來

Come

Help the puppy finds his owner

Come!

Cantonese: heoi3
Mandarin: qù

Go

Choose the right path

 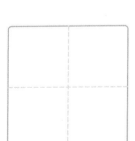  

GO   GO   GO   GO   GO

Ravi

Write the Chinese characters below.

NORTH

WEST

EAST

SOUTH

COME
GO

Cantonese: sek6
Mandarin: shí

1 →
2
4 →
3
5 →

Stone

Color the stones

Cantonese: tin4
Mandarin: tián

Color the animals

1 2
4
3
5

- Farm
- Field

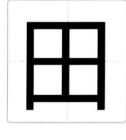
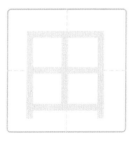

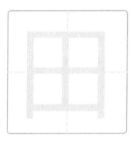

Cantonese: gwo2
Mandarin: guǒ

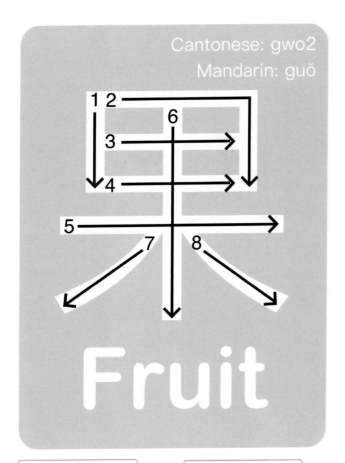

Fruit

Draw your favorite fruits

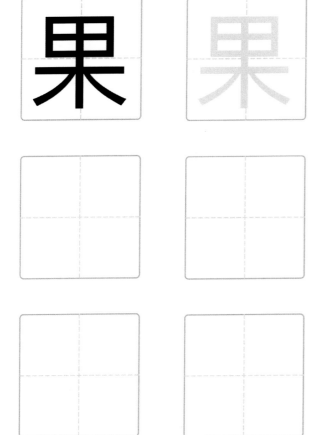

Cantonese: faa1
Mandarin: huā

Flower

Color the flowers

花

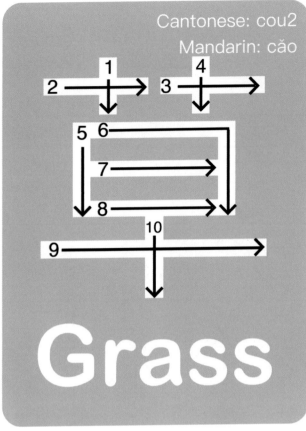

Cantonese: cou2
Mandarin: cǎo

Grass

Color the grass

 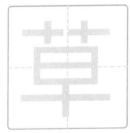  

Cantonese: ho4
Mandarin: hé

River

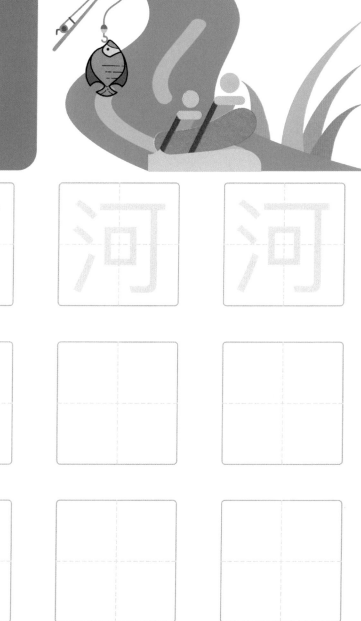

河　河　河　河

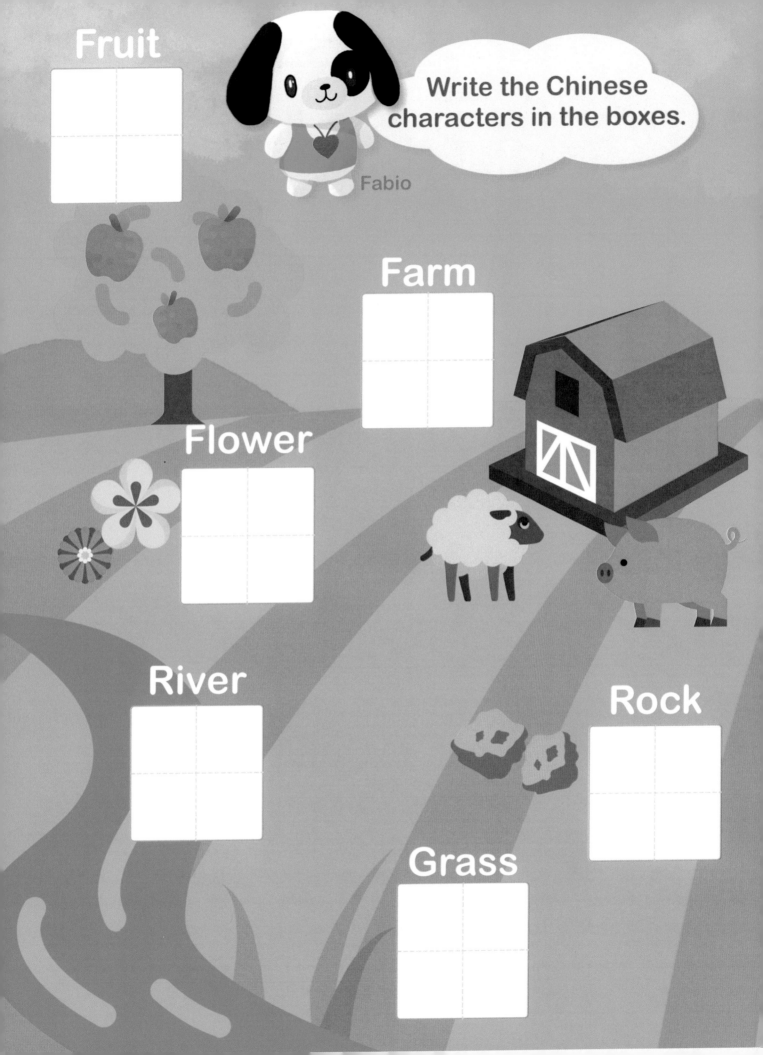

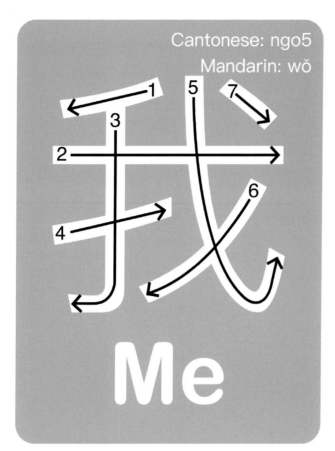

Cantonese: ngo5
Mandarin: wǒ

Me

List 2 fun facts
about yourself

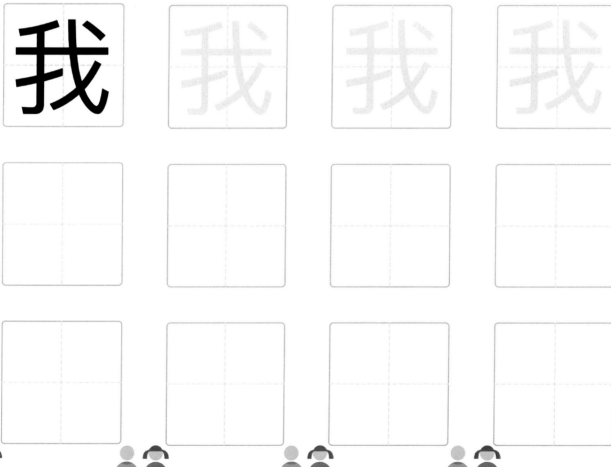

Cantonese: nei5
Mandarin: nǐ

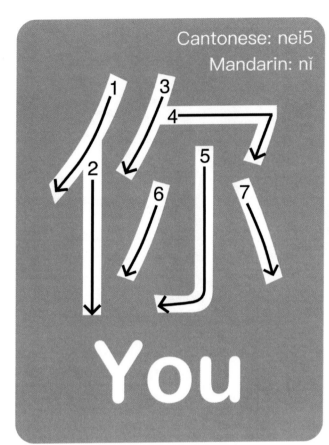

You

What is the secret code?

 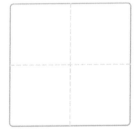  

Cantonese: taa1
Mandarin: tā

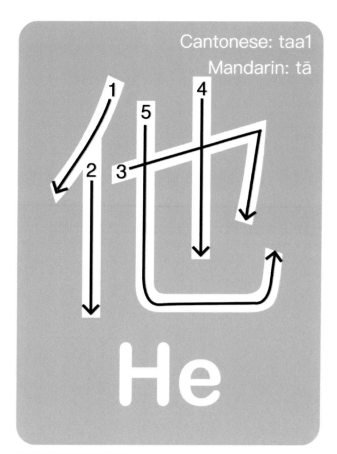

He

Color the boy

他

Cantonese: taa1
Mandarin: tā

She

Color the girl

Draw your Dad

Cantonese: baa1
Mandarin: bà

Dad

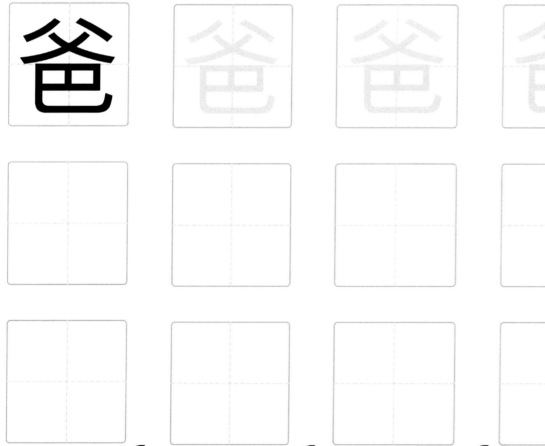

Date : _____

Draw your Mom

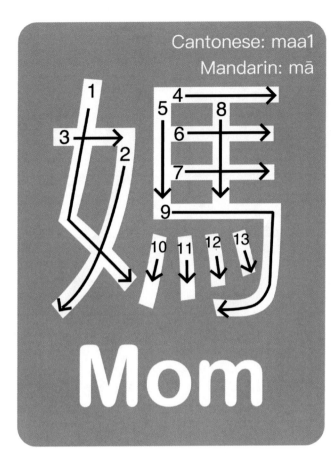

Cantonese: maa1
Mandarin: mā

Mom

媽

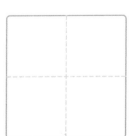

Cantonese: go1
Mandarin: gē

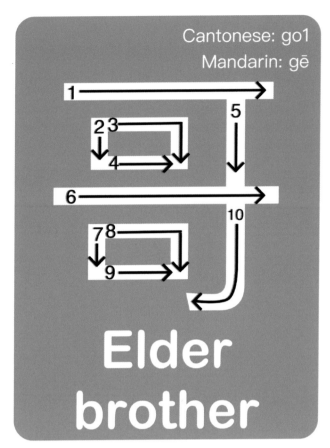

Elder brother

Circle 哥哥

☆☆☆☆☆☆ Date : _____

Cantonese: zi2
Mandarin: zǐ

Elder sister

Circle 姊姊

姊 姊 姊 姊

Cantonese: mui6
Mandarin: mèi

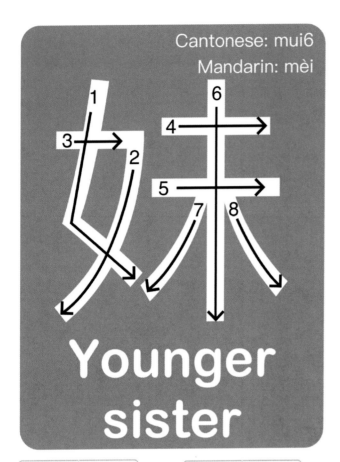

Younger sister

Circle 妹妹

妹

Cantonese: dai6
Mandarin: dì

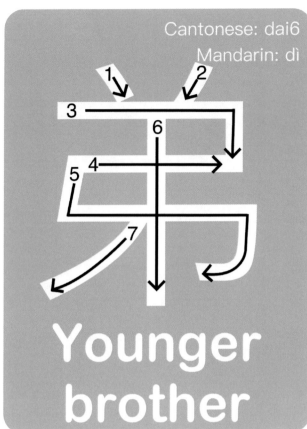

Younger brother

Circle 弟弟

Draw your home

Cantonese: gaa1
Mandarin: jiā

- Home
- Family

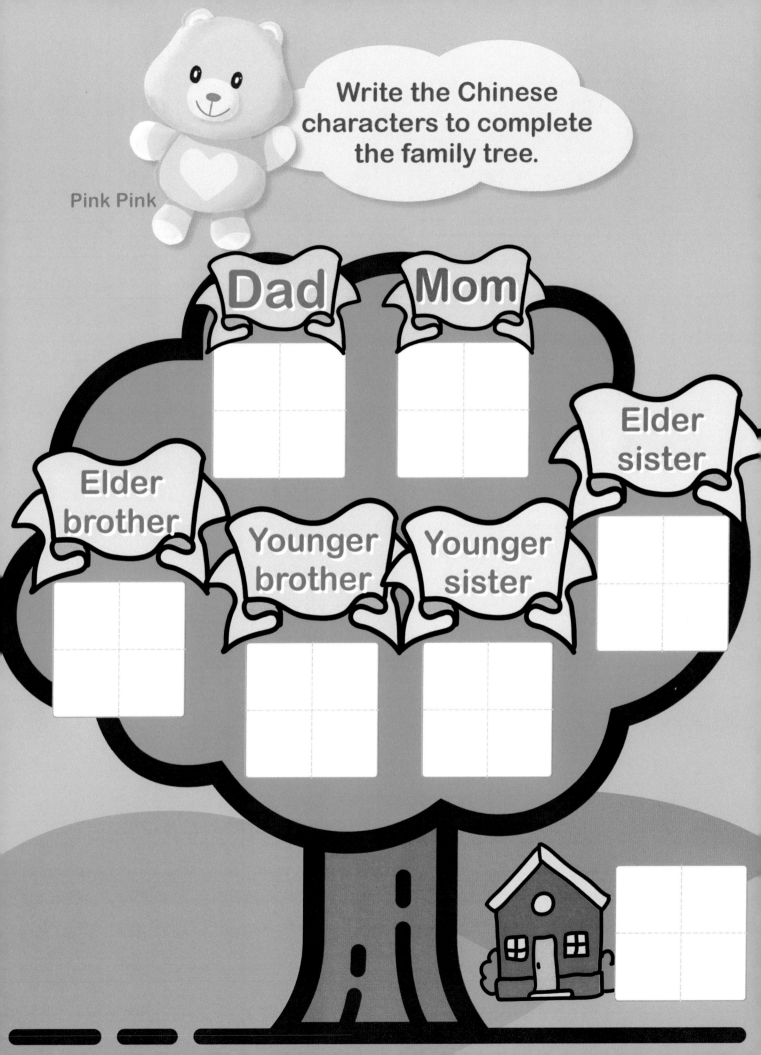

Cantonese: ceon1
Mandarin: chūn

Spring

Color the flowers

Date : _____

Cantonese: haa6
Mandarin: xià

Summer

Draw your favorite summer activities

夏　夏　夏　夏

Color the leaves

Cantonese: cau1
Mandarin: qiū

秋
Autumn

秋

Cantonese: dung1
Mandarin: dōng

1
2
3
4
5

Winter

Give snowman a
pair of mittens

冬

  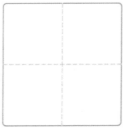 

Date : _____

Cantonese: sing1
Mandarin: xīng

Star

Color the stars

Cantonese: jyu5
Mandarin: yǔ

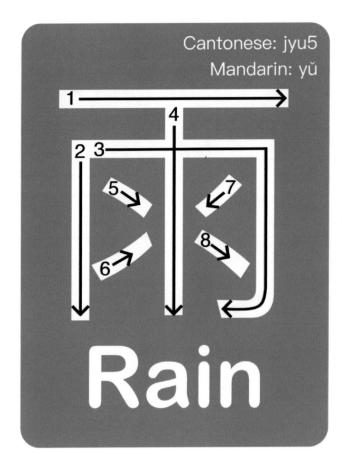

Rain

Color the raindrops

Cantonese: wan4
Mandarin: yún

Cloud

雲

Cantonese: syut3
Mandarin: xuě

Draw a snowman

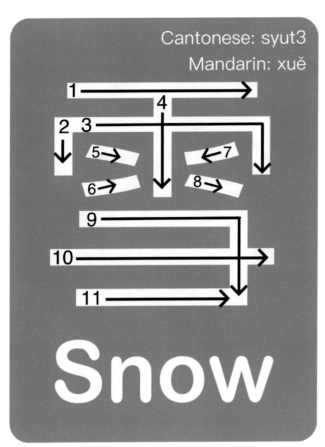

Snow

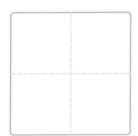

Cantonese: fung1
Mandarin: fēng

Wind

Color the windmill

 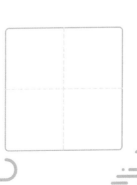  

It's time to practice.
Let's complete the list.

East	South

West	North	Come	Go	Stone	Farm

Fruit	Flower	Grass	River	Me	You

He	She	Dad	Mom	Elder brother	Elder sister

Younger sister	Younger brother	Home	Spring	Summer	Autumn

Winter	Star	Rain	Snow	Wind	Cloud

Made in the USA
Las Vegas, NV
28 September 2023

78274887R00024